PRAISE FOR
THE ODDS OF BECOMING OURSELVES

Carol has a wonderful way of putting both her thoughts and feelings into words. Sometimes her poems are whimsical, sometimes deeply serious. Often they are somewhere in between. With that in mind, as you pick up this book and choose a poem to read, one thing will always be the same. No matter what subject Carol has chosen for a poem, no matter its mood or style, you can be sure that reading it will be a pure joy.

—Dan Cox

Wow! A thrill-packed poem if there ever was one! First-time to white-water rafting must absolutely read this one!

—Vernon King

I really enjoy the poem, *Gershwin on My Mind and You.* I love the integration of the titles of Gershwin's music with the mood and flow of Carol's poem. It would be tragic for this poetry to pass into obscurity. This poem will be appreciated by many. I thank you.

—Kim Forbes Gayton, Paralegal

Love, Love, Love this. I'm still such an excitement junky that I lived through every one of your words and enjoyed the "Ride' Immensely! !
Whooooppeee! Thank you,

—Stephenie "Stevie" Hurlburt

Ms. March is a new poet whose words develop an experience, capture an emotion and invite the reader to become part of the poem. The musicality of playfulness of some of her poems made me hum as I was reading. Great fun!

—Lynn Mullins

The wonderful poems in *The Odds of Becoming Ourselves* represent a lifetime of love, pain and growth for its author, Carol Shelton March. Carol takes the reader into the past she endured as a young wife and mother. She then tells us to "hang on" as her raft meets the waves and Class IV rapids of the Rio Grande whitewater; courage is required for both kinds of life passages.

—Sandra Schackel, PhD. Professor of Women's History (retired) Boise State University

THE
ODDS OF BECOMING
OURSELVES

命

THE
ODDS OF BECOMING
OURSELVES

POETRY AND PROSE MEMOIR

CAROL SHELTON MARCH

The Odds of Becoming Ourselves
Copyright ©2017 Carol Shelton March

ISBN: 978-1-940769-82-0
Publisher: Mercury HeartLink
Silver City, New Mexico
Printed in the United States of America

Cover etching: "Kiss Me My Sweet"
JanetYagoda@gmail.com

The inscription at the beginning of the book and on page 155,
represents "Destiny", a work in concrete by
Albuquerque artist, Peggy Plumb.

Contact the author at:
carolvisits@msn.com

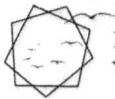

Mercury HeartLink
www.heartlink.com

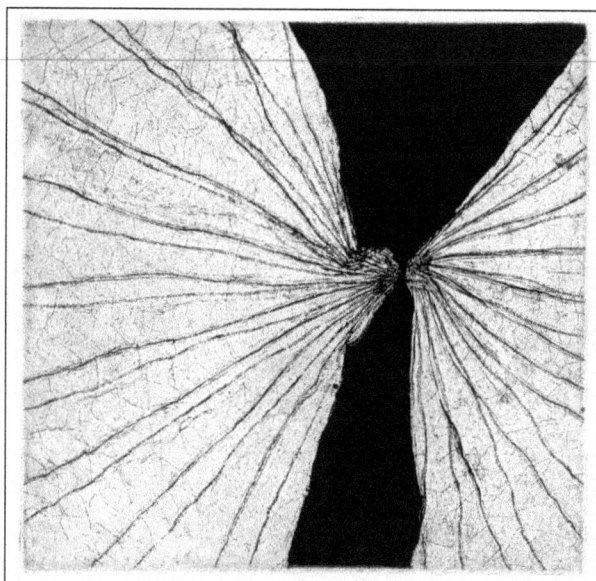

front cover etching
"Kiss Me My Sweet"

Janet Yagoda Shagam

My goal is to give viewers an entryway into contemplative moments—serious, humorous, or even a little white noise. It's all okay! Printmaking has the reputation of being an exacting art. A well-mapped plan. Squared edges. Perfect registration. Pristine results. I have to say I find it difficult to conform to these standards. While I may approach my work with an idea in mind, I welcome the fluidity that comes with wandering thoughts, wonderment and surprise. My work is in collections throughout the United States as well as in Korea, Israel, Africa, and Germany.   —JYS

Contents

PRAISE FOR
THE ODDS OF BECOMING OURSELVES   II

DEDICATION   XVII

SECTION ONE

Not Much to Ask	3
After the Rain	4
The Pull	6
Self Talk	8
Who Are We Who Am I	9
Health Wise	11
Hello Albuquerque	12
Here and Now	13
Body and Brain	16
A Kick Out of You	17
Choosing	18
Inscrutable	19
Details	22
In Love	23
I Can See Why	24
Beyond Description	26
After Thought	28
Junko	29
What Are People For	30

SECTION TWO

Summer at My Grandparents' Cottage   35
A Car Ride   36
In Hot Water   37
An Uphill Climb   40
When I Was A String Bean
     On The Way to Pike's Peak   46
Dream On … A Poem   48

SECTION THREE

A Happy Teen   52
Nature of the Beast   54
Bully Groom   55
Understanding   57
Getting to Know Me   58
Young Married Life   60
Change   61
What Might Have Been   63
Barriers   64

SECTION FOUR

Anchoring   71

SECTION FIVE

Sabotage   79
Jam Sessions 1960s   80
Civil Rights   81
One Love   83
Johnsel   85
Montana Man   86
In the Moment   89

SECTION SIX

With Him   95

SECTION SEVEN

Gershwin On My Mind and You   105
A Puzzlement   108
Arts and Crafts Fair 1970s   109
Juju   111
Light Bulb   112
Lots of Sleep   113
Disquietude   114
Love Me Love Me Knot   115
Bitter Potion   117
Sucker   118
Statuesque   120

Residual Sentiments   122

Not Speaking   123

Magician   125

SECTION EIGHT

Meaning of 9/11   131

Iliana   132

Roosevelt Park   135

Betty   136

Hot Flash Look Out   137

Silently   139

Silly Question   140

Thursday Night Senior Dance   141

Your Dance   143

From My 8th Floor North Window   144

Seeming   145

Why   146

Do You See   150

Addicts   152

How I See You   153

Quiet Curiosity   154

ABOUT THE AUTHOR   157

In memory of my very loving husband
John Abe March Jr. who loved New Mexico
almost as much as Montana.

SECTION ONE

Not Much to Ask

Gimme…lots o' butter on my muffin
Sauce on my pasta
Honey in my tea
I want
Syrup on my pancakes
Spice in disagreements
Flavor in my song
Depth in my prayer
Peaceful thoughts
My neighbors friendly
My lover passionate
My garden lively but calming

I want
Hype in my step
Laughter in my ears
Sunshine in my soul
To know that mommas are kissin' their babies
A thoughtful and seasoned grandpa for the kids
I'd like
Satisfaction in a place
Sweetness in the land
A settled heart
Feisty friends
I want……..
The Whole Enchilada

After the Rain

Morning's first view
a cheery Technicolor sight
feelings of joy the escort

Scent is young
nature sounds vibrant
all is primary and a bit mysterious

Quite a journey from yesterday
when in-your-face parched landscapes
languid at best may have elicited pity

But for now...

The High Desert equalizer
with style of its own
unveils a softly jubilant rainbow

Mountain majesty purple
desert sand sunset
a morning-glory blue sky

All the New Mexico sphere

A musical composition struts
a war bonnet Apache Plume
toward it's peaceful cotton-like blossoms

Indian Rice Grass, Russian Olive branches
bow to a squishy yield at the bank of the Rio Grande
Chamisa hugs the roadside

All meld harmoniously the passage

After the Rain

THE PULL

O the pull
Of the keyboard
The piano no
The poetry pull
The idea dump

The stump
The dig
Dig down
Deep dive
Find more   Find more   Find more

Give rise
Next line
In time
Come
Near

The heart
The soul
The search
The words
O the Pull

Wrong Generation
You like rap
You're 77
Who are you

Where are you
What are you

Doing music
Dancing
Sliding
Poeting
Crazy

What is this mis-step

Self Talk

You say you don't like the person you are becoming
Your life personality through thick and thin
Has been upbeat pleasant and congruent
A strong value has been that your inner self
And who you portray to the outside world correspond

Do your attitudes now reflect your early age environment
The community norms and habits from a vulnerable age
Were you used to a densely populated city
A small town atmosphere where you interact and
Pretending cannot be successful

Is it against your very core to put on an act
As you interact with others do you feel genuine
<u>Are</u> you genuine - no pretending - not counterfeit
Are you in control of your life yet others-oriented
Are you continuing a path of life satisfaction

In the present you live to explore
A more satisfying growth pattern
You succeed in not feeling trapped
Free Free Free At Last!

Who Are We Who Am I

There are Gerontologists
Who say
As we age we become
More ourselves

What?
For some of us
That could be a ghastly idea
Do we have a say

Say what?
Who are we
Self examination
Who am I

So begs the question
Do we submit
Be ourselves
Knowing this

Do we have the power
To repel this phenomena
The capability to examine
The self within us

Are we satisfied with
Who we are now
If not can we
Repel the ghosts

Celebrate the angels
Create new attitudes
Find the bliss or
Find ourselves stuck

This is our big question
Shall we become more
Of who we already are
Or settle for that other person?

Health Wise

Walking
A stroll a day
Missed?
A toll to pay

Makar,
Carol

HELLO ALBUQUERQUE

Hello Albuquerque
Hello my little town
Land of enchantment
Land of sweet diversity
Land where I can look out
My north window and see
Almost forever in the distance
The Jemez Mountains
The Sangre de Christos
The Sandia Mountain Range
Look down upon an October
Sea of colorful treetops
Look up to a blue, blue sky with
Invitations from every cloud formation
Glance left to the west mesa
To face Nine Mile Hill
Where the lights of Albuquerque
At dusk inspired a song

Here and Now

In conversation
Discipline calls
To be in the present
Not in the past

To find new memories
Ones to enjoy
Ones today
Not in the past

The cherished
Remembrances
Held in our hearts
Will not fly away

So what's the point
In over-reliving them
Day after day
Fear they won't stay?

For here for now
We smile say hello
Converse in new ways
With new friends

We create
New experiences
New adventures
New memories

Listening to the present
Living in the present
Being here
Being in the now

Yet continuing
To cherish
To honor and respect
Our memories

Our quality
Of life day to day
Reflects our values
Forever

As well as today
In the Moment
Talk About
Now
Or
Then

Now
Reflects
Today
Yesterdays
Have
Been

One
Can
Take
Refuge
In
Reflecting
The
Past

When
In
The now
Now
Moments
Will
Last.

Body and Brain

Now you
belong to me
you disappeared
for a short while
now you are
mine
again
no more
wondering
no more fright
here we are
back together
you
my body
and brain
you
day
and
night.

A Kick Out of You

It's a song
but right now
I'm going to apply
it elsewhere

                right strait to you
                and our playfulness
                with words

as if we are playing
in a sandbox
at age three
a giggle here
a giggle there

                an email
                back and forth
                belly laughs
                from the heart
                on and on

Choosing

Who
does
the
choosing

What
happens
then

When they choose me
Or when I choose them

INSCRUTABLE

Inspired by these words:
"Boys cry, cigarettes do kill, parents lie, boats sink, flowers
die. Life goes on, with or without you." —anonymous

Flowers may die
some may die
others thrive again
flourish in a new season.
Life, that's another thing.
If we made a plan
where people died
each season
then re-surfaced
the next year
as plants do
how might that
make a difference
in how humans
renew themselves?

Not like boats – sink
and that's it! What life
does a boat have?

Boats sink and they lie there
dead to the outside world.
But down there, say, in the deep
blue sea, they begin

in stages, to rot.
Oh it may be pleasant for them
in the beginning. It's nice and cool,
not like when the sun used to
shine on them causing their skin to peel.
Down in the deep
in the ocean bottom
they find it even more
interesting than
above water
or harbored
on land
with just their
tails in the water.

"Boys cry?"
Of course they do
just like everyone else
except in some cases
where they cannot
where life has been
too hard
unfair.

When babes
in arms
feel burdened
too young
precious
little boys

left
without
a role
model
to fend
to be brave
don't cry
cannot cry.

Some use cigarettes
Some don't
They cry inside
Sink above water.

Parents lie
Say I do
Then don't.

DETAILS

She
likes
to care
in detail
for friends
for dwellings
family and pets
home and dishes
bedding and music
songs and art objects
planting and gardening
then who can forget cars
all vehicles including trucks
old and new tattered and torn
her soft spot is for the early born
where caring and details signal love
there is the affection of soft kid gloves

In Love

Did you fall…
In love?
Are you in love?
Is that what happens?
You fall?
Do you trip and fall?

What is falling in love?
You fall in love with a person?
How is that different from loving someone?
Are you in love?
Or do you love that someone?
"I love you"
….what does that mean?
If you fall does that mean you cannot get up?
Was it an accident? You didn't mean to?
It wasn't on purpose – it just happened?
Now what?
Does it transform?
If not... what?
If so… what?

If you fall in love
Can you fall out?

I Can See Why

His cabinet members
his staff, his advisors
the people who have
an ongoing work
relationship with him
have a multitude
of questions as to the
mental state
mental capacity
mental ability
mental reality

to think beyond himself
as our president of the
United States of America

Many citizens of the
United States of America
are led to ask the same
question observed at one
nation-wide women's
march with a bottom line
that read, "Melania, blink twice
if you want us to save you!"

Would the new cabinet members
of our elected government be
thinking they need a poster
of their own? How would
it read? What would it say?

Beyond Description

At the site
of the imperial purple
a deep violet pouf
radiates over the
expanding landscape
where a lime green
color begins to
slowly resemble
the green of an olive
and a mellow yellow
transmogrifies to a
grotesque burgundy state

The core of the color
spreads in the short run
to the embodiment
of the space while
spawning various
shades and forms
as it decolorizes
into natural flesh

With imagination
the above
description
might transport

you to a mesa
sunset near a
mossy
rocky mountain site

Reality
in the
aftermath
of a major
garage floor slip
it is a
description
over time
of my elbow
knee
and
hip.

After Thought

Pardon me
if you feel
disheartened
at the
misstep
I've
described
but
my
belated
sense
of humor
giving
credence
to the scene
helped me
to realize
you
might
know
just
what
I mean.

JUNKO

A little Junko
Plays cat
And mouse
With a kitten

A novice
The kitten
It's clear
To the bird

The Junko
Turns
Toward
The kitten

Takes flight
Observes
From a lower branch
And the game goes on…

WHAT ARE PEOPLE FOR

People are for loving
caring if you will
recognizing others
on their path or journey still
why is there such hatred
such blame and seeming plight
hope is the savior
dare we stay the fight

People are for high regard
regardless of their being
history the lesson
what problems can be seen
everything is fine I've been told
but my great, great, great
grandmother wasn't sold

People are for connecting
despite their different ways
requiring understanding
empathy...we now realize
sometimes we don't hear it
native people were colonized

People are for what
not for losing hope
turn plight into a problem
to use an Alinsky quote
problems find solutions
joined together there is power
a fate worse than death he says
is giving up the hour.

SECTION TWO

Summer at My Grandparents' Cottage

On the path to the outhouse
I don't know
Who tries to capture me
The most...
The Bumble Bees
Or the thorns
On the Rose Bushes

One pretends
To be busy
The other sits still
Ready for the bait
That's the situation
As I try to come up
With a strategy

A Car Ride

What a nice summer weekend day it is
for everyone to be outside in Johnson City
Tennessee; especially wonderful if you are
four years old like my little brother Ronnie.
On this particular day children are romping
in the grass. Neighbors have gathered
their children round while moms are
preparing for a picnic in the yard and dads
are relaxing for the weekend vacation.

Everyone seems to be very pleased with all
the fun they are having and are very much
into the activities of the day when suddenly
the tide turns. Ronnie is nowhere in sight.
We search all over the yard. We look inside
our house and the neighbors' houses while my
dad walks across the street to search. None
of us could find Ronnie anywhere. My dad
decides to take the car and drive all around
the block to look for him.

Meanwhile much to our surprise Ronnie
re-appears. Stooping down close to him
my mother says gently, "Young man,
do you know that your daddy is looking
all over this neighborhood for you?"
Ronnie looked at her, tears welling up
and said, "I wanted to go with him."

In Hot Water

Every time I ran my bath water I made it extra hot.
I started taking my bath on my own when I was five.
That was when I decided to train myself to be tough
even in very, very, hot water.I did this to save myself.
I made the decision on my own. Nobody helped me
and I kept it to myself. I knew if I could get used to
very hot water and the Nazis came to torture me,
I would cry out, "Whatever you do, don't put me in a
tub with really hot water."I would trick the Nazis into
thinking that hot water torture would be the worst
thing they could do to me. So I practiced it every
time I took a bath. I would fill the bath tub as full
as I could. I'd get undressed, take a big deep breath,
and step into the tub. I'd let my feet get used to the
water first, and then I'd sit down in the hottest water
I could stand all the way up to my neck. After a little
While when the water would start to cool, I'd let some
of the water drain out and I'd turn the hot water faucet
on again to let more hot water into the tub.

Who are the Nazis anyway? Only thing I knew was
that they were bad. When I lived in Tennessee and
walked home from first grade every day, I didn't stay
on the sidewalk. It was lots more fun to walk on top
of the concrete wall next to the sidewalk. In case I
would accidently fall my brother Jerry would be
walking home from his school not far behind me.
I knew if I fell he would help me get up and we could

walk the rest of the way home together. Before second grade started our family moved a long way from Tennessee to Wisconsin. Walking home there was an adventure too. It got really cold and snowed a lot. The snow got so deep you couldn't even see the sidewalks. Workers had dug paths in the deep snow and that's where little kids walked to school. And even though the sides of the cave-like paths were taller than the kids, it was the only place they had to walk to school. As you walked along you could look to the right and to the left. But no matter what, you couldn't see anything but the two sides of the snow packed walls.
You had to just keep walking straight ahead.
Then when spring came it got slushy on the paths and the walls melted away.
The sidewalk appeared again. As it got warmer you could start skipping along your way.

One day when I was on my way home from school I saw a design that somebody had made on the sidewalk with chalk. I couldn't tell what it was supposed to be, or if it was writing, printing, or some kind of picture. I took a pencil and a piece of paper out of my school bag right there and made a drawing just like the one on the sidewalk. The design I made with my pencil was almost as big as my tablet – it barely fit on the sheet of paper. The one on the sidewalk was even bigger. It wasn't hard to draw. All you had

to do was make a few lines in different directions.
I finished my drawing in a few minutes and started
again on my way home.

My mother's cooking was the best in the world.
I could tell what she was cooking for supper that day.
You could smell her delicious tasting spaghetti and
meat sauce as you got close to our porch. I opened
the screen door. I walked past my brother's pet
snakes on the porch in the wooden Velveeta boxes
and put my school bag and stuff in the pass-through
just outside the other side of the kitchen. We had
supper at 6:30 after my dad got home from work.
That's what time we had supper every night. On that
night, after we finished the dishes and cleaned up
the kitchen, I got my tablet out and showed my family
the drawing I copied from the sidewalk. I don't
remember all the words my daddy said, but suddenly
everything turned awful when he said, "Don't ever
draw that again." I didn't know what I did wrong.
After I tore up my drawing and threw it in the kitchen
waste basket, I went back to the porch. For a little
while I talked to Jerry's pet snakes in their nice and
cozy wooden Velveeta box that had a piece of a
screen door for a roof. Then I put my Betty Grable
and June Haver paper dolls to bed and said good night.
I didn't know my drawing was a Swastika.
I didn't know what that was.

AN UPHILL CLIMB

They called it
The *Flexible Flyer*
Jerry age 10
Had never seen

He had heard the talk
The grown-up talk
But the *Flyer* ...
A secret it seemed

Would it be in the garage
Maybe that's a clue
It could be there somewhere
Witnessed by only a few

When he would get older
He thought perhaps bolder
He'd investigate
In secret if true

High on an inside
Unfinished wall
Something out of
Reach was suspect

A mysterious bundle
With a rope tied canvas
For safety measures
One might expect

Jerry was puzzled
At the tightly wrapped
Clump that appeared
To be close to his height

As wide as his arm
Length - three feet
He guessed… possible
But maybe not quite

Jerry looked closely
At the nails that held
The bundle he supposed
For its protection

If it were to juggle
In a slightly wrong way
It could fall
Who knows in what direction

He wondered how heavy
Or light it would be
If he could get it down
Off the wall just to see

But fearful of getting in trouble
So far it was his secret mission
Then on second thoughts Jerry had
He decided to ask for permission

Carefully he asked the question
"The bundle hanging
In storage Dad, what is it
Some kind of contraption"

To Jerry's surprise being just a kid
Dad said, "Let's take a look"
Into the garage they ventured
'Till they came to just the right place

Oh that, Dad said, I'll show you
Now that you're old enough
It is something I know you'll enjoy
Hence the smile on Jerry's face

Winter around the corner
Couldn't have been better timing
The discovery Jerry had pursued
Was a *Flexible Flyer* trimmed in red

What next he thought, what does it mean
My knowledge that the package holds a sled
All I can do is hope for the best
Wash, brush my teeth, go to bed

I'll need to go by all the rules
Do exactly as I'm told
I know my dad has lots of those
I think I know exactly what to say

There are rules about choosing friends
I have to keep in mind
My Dad gave me a lecture one time
About with whom I'm to play

Hope I can take the *Flyer*
To a place nearby I've seen
It's a wonderful snowy steep hill
I could go sledding after school

Another thing was on Jerry's mind
He had to think hard about
Once allowed to take the sled
His father had a very strict rule

In no uncertain terms, Dad said
"Don't let anyone else use this sled."
You'd think Jerry had a dilemma
But he was quick you might also guess

When a little boy came up to him
And asked, "Could I borrow your sled
Next ride down the hill "Jerry paused
For not even a minute said, "Yes"

The two little boys on that first day
New companions took turns on the sled
Jerry had made his own decision and
Took actions that taught him a lesson

Father knows best, not always
It's never too early to learn
A mind of your own is beneficial
Despite those who think it's rebellion

Jerry ignored the warnings
Two that he recalled
In no uncertain terms, said our father
"Don't let anybody use this sled."

Precisely there was another rule, Jerry remembers well
"If I ever catch you playing with a N****r kid
I'm going to whip the daylights out of you."
That was the warning, that's what was said.

Jerry must have had plenty of fun
Breaking strict and discriminatory rules
To him a kid was a kid
Jerry made no distinction

Thinking for himself at an early age
And keeping this noteworthy secret
The joy he must have felt throughout
Hooray! Jerry turned another page

Partners in crime now friends
Sharing fun every ride down the hill
The little boy sharing the *Flyer*
Was a black child Jerry's same age

You might like to know
And I'd like to tell you
When my brother first
Told me this story

'Twas in his 80th year
A secret he had protected
Told to me with brotherly love
And modest pride and glory

When I Was A String Bean
On The Way to Pike's Peak

My dad hollered, "Get in the car kids,
we're going to Pikes Peak!"
My mother and I were both secretly reluctant
About driving to Pikes Peak from Southwest Missouri
My mother and I, you could say, were buried in our own
Home town friends, activities and interests
Didn't need to go out of town for entertainment
But in an era of *Father Knows Best*
We hopped in our 1951 Ford four-door sedan
Headed north and west - first stop Kansas City
At a car wash where passengers
Remain in their car while workers wash it
My little brother was sitting in the back seat with me
When a young boy about my age, 13 or 14,
was washing our car
Our eyes met when I looked out
the car window at him and
He looked in the car window at me
When our eyes met it was a moment of fascination
My eyes had never seen a person any
other color than white
My memory has always told me that I smiled
at him and he smiled at me
Could it have been my imagination or wishful thinking?
What amazes me about it is how this brief moment that
happened when I was
A young girl has popped up in my memory

over many decades
Those brown-eyes-met-green-eyes-moments, teen-ager to
teen-ager, white to black,
Black to white
Are ones I've cherished

Pikes Peak? Oh yeah, we were there.

Dream On ... A Poem

Loud screams
AAHHHHh!
EEEHHHH!
Elvis is coming to town!!
Blocks away!

Tumultuous on campus
And probably many miles away
The rumble rolled through the
Freshman girls dorm like nothing
Ever heard there before

The anticipation of seeing and hearing
The newly popular Elvis Presley
Was almost more than one could digest
The talk was true ELVIS in concert
In person only two miles away

At least 100 girls from my dormitory
With their tickets in hand left for the concert
That evening - yet for a few of us the interest
In Elvis was lacking – guess we just weren't with it
Even when the concert ended that night

And the girls came running and jumping in the
Front door one scream after another I still
Couldn't get excited – I suppose you could call
Me a dreamer because the music for me in 1955
Equally enticing but much less turbulent

Was the music of Nat King Cole
The album, *Love Songs,* struck every chord in
My listening repertoire – was and is *Unforgetable*
For teens thinking they would someday fall in love
The melodic ballad **When I Fall In Love** suited them

Lyrics to another song were more direct

They tried to tell us we're too young
Too young to really be in love
They say that Love's a word, a word
we've only heard and can't begin to know
the meaning of/ And yet we're not too young
to know/our love may last though years
may go/ and then some day they may recall
we were not too young at all

The album lives today…violins are playing
It takes us to a dream to another place we want
To experience or perhaps takes us back to a sweet
Remembrance, to a certain someone, we can place
Ourselves there at any time in life

This music our guide
But as history goes
Elvis is King!

As for Nat…

Stay As Sweet As You Are

SECTION THREE

A Happy Teen

One day
When I
Was a
Teenager
My mother
Noticed
How happy
I was

Then she
Said to me....
If you think
You are
Happy now
When you
Get married
And have
Children
That's when
You will be
The happiest

I was very
Excited
About
The prospect
Of having
Children

Maybe
That is
What fed
My ambition
At age 18
To get married
And that
Alone

Nature of the Beast

Every incident
from the first
mouth shut
domestic
violence
episode

Comes
out of the blue
no evidence of any
reason except possibly
for entertaining themselves
bully's find ways to exhibit their power

Bully Groom

I'm going to
Keep choking
You until
You say
Please
Stop
Silence…
She said
Nothing
She started
Thinking
If she
Didn't say
Please
Stop
She may
Not
Be able
To
Say it
When it's
Too late
And she
Cannot

She said
"Please stop".
The couple

Got out
Of the car
Walked
To their
Apartment
He said nothing
She said nothing
Silenced...

Understanding

The definition of
Domestic abuse
Takes some thought
It's not about a
Disagreement
An argument
It's about the
Need to show
Power
Over another
Brute power
Bully power
To show
Dominance
And create fear

Getting to Know Me

Stand up for myself?
disallowed
ask questions?
disallowed
have an opinion?
disallowed
in my father's house
you'd be scolded
labeled
questioning
anything
as a child
was considered
disrespectful
so I was labeled
smart-mouth
sassy
I was
far
from
smart-mouth
sassy
I dared not
speak up
got to
realize
I wasn't
smart

now
I know
if you
don't ask
questions
even if you
are a girl
you cannot
be smart - I learned it in college at age 54.

YOUNG MARRIED LIFE

One night at home
When she was quietly
In bed with her husband
He purposely put the
Lit hot-fire end
Of his cigarette
Against her bare skin
He did it for effect
And cruelty

Throughout her life
Into an older age
A reminder is the
Small scar just under
Her right breast

CHANGE

I nursed our sweet
sweet newborn child
kissed his tiny hands
his little forehead
cradled him in my arms
slowly and gently
transferred him
back to his crib

I returned to the kitchen
where you stood leaning against
the counter-top staring at me
a hateful look in your eyes

without a word
continuing your stare
out of nowhere you grabbed
my shoulders and threw me bodily
across the 10 feet width
of the kitchen floor where
I landed on my back against
the floor baseboard and the wall

as this was not the first
abusive incident in our
four year marriage
things had changed
now I am a mother

my responsibilities
are greater than myself
as an individual

greater than cooking your meals
cleaning our rental
quietly tolerating
whatever slap, push
unspeakable mean
behavior you might
at any surprise moment
impose upon me.

WHAT MIGHT HAVE BEEN

Looking back
What if she had said
"No."
What would he
Have done then
Without a divorce

In hindsight
It is an adventure
To suppose
What might have been

They could have
Separated
Not divorced
Could have
Lived apart
Without the abuse

Instead of
Outside work
She could have
Stayed at home

Every day
With her precious
Baby boy

Barriers

To be loved
My children
To know love
To live love
Be cared for
In a loving way
As a parent
Loves their child
And child to parent
In a kind substantial way

To be loved
My children
To know love
To live love
To witness love
Parents one to the other
In a loving manner
Partner to spouse
Parent to child
A healthy shielding path

It wasn't to be
For the silence in me
Led another to show
His power
To me at me
Beside me

A young woman
A wife at 18
And for a time
The bread-winner

A few years passed
A son was born
Months later
The male voice declared
I've decided I no longer want
The responsibility of marriage

Well Waahoo!
A mother
A divorcee
A single mother
I had learned
To be afraid

And then
A time came
When
I Escaped
Escaped the power
Escaped the dominance
Escaped the brutality
Escaped the bullying

Found my own way
A safer more peaceful path

Lived more modestly
My children and me
More whole
Respected
Protected
Strong
Loved
Free

SECTION FOUR

ANCHORING

Waves soared high splashing
five or six feet higher than
Richard's raft. We edged closer
and closer to the ominous
waves near the giant boulders
as Richard shouted, "Carol, Bob,
double check your life vests".
Shut off by the curtain of
crashing waves we could
barely see him could not
hear him could only rely on
his body language as he
motioned to us rechecking
his own life vest more and
more water gushed into the
lower end of our raft as the
high end took the waves
head on the raft would rise
with the wave then descend
rise and descend splashing
water in and out of the ten
person raft the three of us
rode the waves with the front
end high and mighty while
river water blasted and
ricocheted against us the water
itself independently dictated our
direction the waves continued to

toss the raft dangerously close
to the boulders oars were of no use
we were a tilt-a-whirl on the water
snapping from side to side up and
down not knowing which direction
the movement would take us next
or how fast our raft might spin and
be unexpectedly bounced yanked
from one part of the raft to another
all the while hoping we wouldn't spin
into the depths of the river or crash
into the volcanic boulders
suppose you are at the put-in
and this is your first time on
Class IV rapids you're on the river
where you peacefully float along
the river sets the pace soft and
gliding you experience a calm
quiet float in a settled area of the
Rio Grande you relax - smile at
the sun take a nice deep breath
be prepared for the next part
of the ride where you
will be silenced
you cannot communicate
the roar of the river muffles
all other sounds
you see Captain Richard
with the oars you know
he is speaking - shouting

but you cannot hear him
white water continues to
splash in your face
into your eyes
you are in total silence
yet surrounded by
unrestrained noise and
motion for the next several
minutes you'd be riding high
on a giant wave moments later
the pace would speed and you'd
be dropped yes that's the expression
dropped you would have just
survived the drops of three
rapids a relentless stretch
of whitewater a 15-foot
fall down a steep chute
of water is next one
long section of rapids
designation: *Difficult*
a rapid of any status
at all has a specific
designation
rapids also have names
meet *Pinball, Buzz Saw,*
and *Screaming Left Turn*
The Rio Grande River is a
trickster where we
were - at the put-in
it was calm that's where

Richard had me start
with the oars it begins
with a slow ride a gentle float
you lean back and relax the lining
the barriers inside the raft between
you and the water are like huge
black rubber pillows on a giant
featherbed filled with solid air
the slow glide is a lullaby
then suddenly the pace
quickens the drops become
steeper this is the sixteen mile
run of the *Lower Box* in force
where thrill seeking rafters
earn their badge of courage
that's where we were
if you'd been on this ride
would you have wanted
a badge for this
hand me a badge please!
No - hand that badge to Richard
it seemed there was only a slim
chance we could safely float
out of there that's what
it felt like as we had
successfully challenged
the Class IV white water of
New Mexico's portion of the
Rio Grande River
Richard managed

the threat of the rapids
we did - after all - safely float
to the take-out no one had
been thrashed overboard
things were quiet from
there it was smooth
sailing at least for
this day

SECTION FIVE

Sabotage

They call him Sabotage
Useful for his cause
Gains mileage
In his undermining ploy
A monkey wrench
Without pause
Sets out to destroy
To willfully destruct
Yet hidden in the part
This role he does best
That shatters your heart

His tool?
Saccharine
A silken honeyed gambit
With creative maneuvering
Disguised at a fabricated level
He plummets
To the depths of the sea
Where he feels at home
That sly olde devil

Jam Sessions 1960s

Kansas City
Introduction
To Night club
Dancing
To jazz
To afternoons
Evenings
A **segregated**
Public

Afterhours
Attic jams
Jazz lovers
Early morning
Music
All together
Integrated
For the music
With the music

CIVIL RIGHTS

How long will it take?

Haskins coached Basketball
Dees practiced Civil Rights Law
Schooley taught Sunday school
Haskins – Coached first black team to
NCAA National Basketball Championship
Dees - Rights the Wrongs of discrimination
through Civil Court, a precedent
Schooley - Explains, Educates, Enlightens
her class of teens
All knowing
It wouldn't be
A cakewalk
To what purpose
These good people
Who happen to be
White
Progress
Toward equality
Did their work save four little girls?
NO
Have they influenced others?
YES
How?
By example

By continuing
To march on
Through
Stubbornness
And Dedication

King would be pleased

ONE LOVE

Only one love
Where
My brain
My heart
My soul
Engaged me

The one love
The only love
Of mutual
Admiration
John Abe
March

Tonight
On *Colores*
Featuring
Allen Houser
Sculpture
Confirms

Never was
Our love
Stronger
Than the day
The two of us
Watched the film

In the Allen Houser
Gallery
Together
Tearful
At the deep
Meaning

When both
John March
And
Allen Houser
Were still
Very much alive

JOHNSEL

You are the music in my voice
The music in every day
Music to my ears
Music in my life
A deep lasting love melody
The melody plays on
The music is love
Forever in love
My Johnsel

Montana Man

What would life
Be like if you were here
Would I be singing
Would I be dancing
Would I have this
Individuality I've found
Would I have gained the
Confidence I'm wearing now

What would you have
Been like in your older age
Continued to be earnest
Smart, charming, amiable
No doubt you would have
You know what they say ...
We become more ourselves
As we age

Right now I see you smiling
At me the way you always did
Your eyes focused on mine
I see them in our photographs
I've wondered these past 14 years
Would you and I still be trying to
Hold back tears at the evening news

Would we be sitting at breakfast on Central
On a Saturday morning talking about

What we'd be doing, how we'd be surviving
If we ever became homeless
A slim possibility but nevertheless
An interesting exercise

I know you would remember those
Couple of mornings when we had observed
A homeless woman going into the rest room
And coming back out with freshly shampooed hair
When we'd laugh at ourselves saying
"Okay jot that down,
We know where we can get a shampoo."

If you were here now, would you still
Want me to do the driving on a road trip
I know there were at least two reasons
Why you wanted me to drive
For one, you'd been driving around city and
Country showing real estate to clients
You were tired of being behind the wheel
Secondly, you knew I loved to drive cross country

Besides, I wanted to introduce you more
To New Mexico, you Montana Man you
Now when I see a Montana license plate
Still rare, I see you motioning to the driver
In your mischievous way to say,
"Where are you from in Montana?"
The driver might smile and yell back, "Great Falls"
And you, with your giant smile, would yell across the lane,

"I'm from Missoula".
The driver of the other car would ask,
"Do you live in New Mexico now?"
The two of you would carry on the conversation
Smiling and laughing despite traffic.

Dedicated to the Life and Happiness
Of John Abe March   May 31, 1939 – May 18, 2003

In the Moment

Talk
Is
About
Now
Or
Then

Now
Reflects
Today
Yesterdays
Have
Been

One
Can
Take
Refuge
In
Reflecting
The
Past

When
In
The
Now

Now
Moments
Will
Last

SECTION SIX

WITH HIM

He is there
I'm there with him
He stares at
The giant airliner
His youthful
Brown eyes
Open wide

He begins
To grasp
The reality of
His first flight
Destination Ohio
Track meet
Relay team race

With his friend
And team-mate
My son
10/11 year old
Competition
This pair
I chaperone

Patrick with his natural
Woolly black hair
George with his natural
Straight blonde hair

Close friends
Like babes
In my arms

Each choose a seat
Close to the mom
Protector of first flights
Still no guarantee
They won't
Both turn green

At the rising
Of the plane
Which soon
Settles down
To a level pace
Where the two boys
Notice the independence

The strength of the
Other athletes
15/16 year old
Track stars
Winners
What the two younger boys
Are and would someday be

Other young boys - Not so fortunate

He is there
I'm there with him
Suddenly he is in other hands
Five or six others
With the power
With the strength
With the authority
With the license to beat him

He is afraid
I am afraid for him
He fears for his life
I fear for his life
I fear for many lives
His is gone
Another
Five against one
Is N****r fun

He is there
I'm there with him
A 12 year old boy plays at a park
Across the street from his home
He has a plastic replica of a gun
Is shot down by a police officer
His sister runs to aid him
Is tackled by police
As her brother dies

He is there
I'm there with him
The young high school sophomore
Accused of stealing another teen's back-pack
Was told if he would admit to this crime
He would be released
He did not commit the crime
He asked to prove his innocence in court
He was locked up, held prisoner anyway,
though never convicted

Without a trial, yet to be tried
Was sent to an adult federal prison
For three years - 700 of those days
in solitary confinement
At times guards left him to starve
He was beaten by guards and other inmates
He was finally released at age19 and attended college
Twelve days after his 22nd birthday
He wrapped an air-conditioner power cord
Around his neck and hanged himself

He is there
I'm there with him
Suddenly
Unknowingly
He is a target
The young student walks along
On a cool evening

His jacket has a hood
He's in a "safe" neighborhood

The student walks in a store
Typical teenager - buys some snacks
Begins his walk back through
The neighborhood to the home
Where he and his father plan
To watch a basketball game
A vigilante stalks him
Wrestles him to the ground
Shoots and kills him

The young high school student
Eating his snacks as he walks
Has no weapon
Is taken down
Struggles for his life
Dies there on the green grass lawn
Another game
Another gone

He is there
I'm there with him
He lived in Chicago 1955
His mother let him travel to visit
His cousin in Mississippi
One day the two boys bought some candy in a store
He smiled as he paid
They say gave a flirty whistle
To the pretty white woman cashier

Nights later he was abducted by two white men
They took him to a barn tortured and beat him
They gouged out one of his eyes
Before shooting him through the head
Disposed of his body in the Tallahatchie River
Weighting it down with a 70 pound cotton-gin fan
Tied around his neck with barbed wire
His 14 year old body was retrieved
From the bottom of the river, the Tallahatchie River

He is there
I'm there with him
His Mother is there
I'm there with her
She wanted folks to remember
To see what they did to her son
How he drew his last breath
She would endure the pain of seeing him this way
So others would see him in his open casket

And
Guess what?
His spirit is alive.
You cannot beat to death his spirit
You cannot shoot and kill it
You cannot gouge it to death
You cannot drown it

The Spirit of Emmett Till is Alive
And will never die.

Eric Garner   Freddie Gray   Tamir Rice
Kalief Browder   Trayvon Martin   Emmett Till

SECTION SEVEN

Gershwin On My Mind and You

How could I slight
My thinking so much of you
When everyday I'm singing
Gershwin love songs and blues

In the Gershwin melody
"Just Bidin' My Time"
I'm in a dream land and
Oh soooo sublime

"I've Got a Crush On You"
And I cannot deny it
Since we've been acquainted
This heart's anything but quiet

Gershwin said it
"Somebody Loves Me, I wonder who?"
I'm the someone wondering
Could it by chance be you?

And could it be I'm disheartened
**"They're Singing Songs of Love
But Not for Me"** Gershwin's words
Shall I make them my plea?

What about my yearning for closeness
"Embrace Me, My Sweet Embraceable You"
We've spoken of this affection
Warm delightful hugs for two

Together looks like, acts like
We've got a certain rhythm
A *"Fascinatin' Rhythm"*
Yet we haven't even danced

Dance? No, *"I Got Rhythm"*
Perhaps take another tack
No matter what we do
May be we would never look back

Or one of us might take the attitude
"Let's Call the Whole Thing Off"
That would settle it easily
One or both of us aloft

Both realizing within us
We may not have that feeling
"I Got Plenty of Nuttin'"
You know, but with a lovey-dovey rrring!

Yet here I go on second thoughts
"They Can't Take That Away From Me"
Those sweet memories are in the way
Either we do or don't, leave or stay

Your words always sound so sweet
When you say, *"Lady Be Good"*
In my dreams in that city
Make believe city I know I could

I know what I've got
"I've Got Rhythm"
I've Got Music
And here it comes again

Who Could Ask for Anything More?
Who Could Ask For Anything more!

note: Sing the **bold lines** *if you like.*

A Puzzlement

You do things
Without thinking
Because
You've just
Always
Done them

Without thinking
You do things
You've always
Done them
Just
Because

You've always done
Them
Without thinking
Just because
You
Do things

Arts and Crafts Fair 1970s

Jackie, a talented macramé artist Invited me to
help her at her booth to show and sell her unusual
creations when a strong wind began to sweep the
grounds. Unforgiving gusts roared into the tent booths
fair goers, artists, and guests began to run for cover
while accompanying me that day was my 10 year old
son George who seemed to love the activity of merchants,
customers and sellers, potters and painters and
the colorful magic wonder of artists creating
their work.

As the wind gusts on the fairgrounds settled to
a quiet breeze, my son George, explorer, ambitious
10 year old treasure hunter had walked a few booths
down from our booth station with Jackie to a trash
barrel where several artists had tossed their damaged art

A transparent look of joy on his little face, eyes open wide,
 he said, "Mom, look at this broken pottery I found in that
big trash barrel". Oh my gosh George, that piece is the
distinguished work of Rick Dillingham. He must be very
upset, distraught, that this wonderful piece of art is
missing. It must have blown off his display into the
trash but of course, we can't keep it. When the wind
dies down you and I can return the pottery to the artist.

The next few minutes George was in deep thought
as he revisited our conversation. He might have been

thinking he should keep it since he had discovered it in the trash. So at the dissipation of the wind George and I walked together to the Dillingham booth. George held the pottery piece lovingly and carefully in his hands as he prepared to give it up. "Hello, my son found this pot in the big trash barrel over there and wishes to return it to you.

Distraught indeed, Rick, his head shaking
as he looked down,waved it off
and said,"You can keep it."George and I both
commented, are you sure?
It is such a wonderful work of art, can it be
repaired?Yes the artist/potter said.
You may keep it. George said
in a very thoughtful and mannerly way,
Thank you very much. We hugged
Mr. Dillingham, expressed appreciation for the beauty
of his art. An appreciation of art,
George held the damaged pot as he said,
"Mom, I'll sell the pot to you for $10."

JUJU

A woman at your side
On command
Though tacitly
Something you wear
And wear well
You wear her well
A lucky charm

You
Masked in confidence
Your arrogance
Clear
As she better understands
Her role
Of Mascot

LIGHT BULB

In moments of stress
Everyday living
Preoccupation
There will occasionally
Be a little slip
You don't always
Remember things
Perfectly
No one does.
Turning off the lamp
At the base
Of the lamp
Or at the switch
On the cord
You paid it no matter
Just turned it off
It's not a dumb thing
Or a smart thing
It just is.
How important is that?
The light bulb works.

LOTS OF SLEEP

She slept with him in five different homes
Hers, his, theirs, his, hers
He slept with her in five different homes
Hers, His, Theirs, his, hers
They slept together in their Friends' homes
They slept together in their Families homes

They slept together on the East coast
Slept together In Rhode Island
In Connecticut
In New Jersey
In Massachusetts
In Vermont

They slept together up the Coast Line of California
Slept together at San Luis Obispo
In Nevada
In Colorado
In Arizona
In Taos

They slept together in Beijing
Slept together in Shanghai

And_they slept together in
Truth or Consequences

DISQUIETUDE

Her heart is naive
Her soul the same
Brain mimes
Falls in line
Justifies
The numbness

On occasion
A strong moment
Her brain kicks in
Rebels
Marches in step
With its own values

It's a constant war of the parts
One wins one loses
The other wins the other loses
Her query
When will they be in sync
Where is the win/win

Love Me Love Me Knot

When you tell
Me that I say
"I love you"
Too much

What does
That say about you
And what does
It say about me

In the excitement
Of the moment
Especially when we've
Not been together
For awhile
I say with
Great enthusiasm
"I Love You"

Are you thinking
You should say it back
But cannot
Is guilt in your heart
That you don't
Feel love for
Either of us
Me or you

Bridges are there for burning
Pages are there for turning

Inspired by J. Croce

BITTER POTION

Like a poison on steroids
He drowns in his own venom
Entrenchment surrounds his cave

Inside
The barbed wire of narcissism
Strangles him from head to toe
Getting too close will entangle your emotions
And swirl you into the depths of the sea

His cave resides there
It's a place where small leaches, little by little
Suck the blood slowly out of your senses
One meaningless conversation after another
Until you have died a thousand times over

As your blood turns to ice

Sucker

I know why
You want me
You want to suck
Out the blood of
My positives
You take what you want
What satisfies a need
Then you're gone
Yes you'll be back
But not until
Again you have
Temporarily
Run out
Of new sources
Yes back to me
Over and over
Back to me
You are a spider
A snake
Looking for
Fresh prey
A renewed victim
Ripe again
To be lifted up
Then dropped

Don't mess with
My happiness
Not again….
Please!

STATUESQUE

There
It Is
That
Straight
Ahead
Stare
Stone
Face
Shoulders
Upright
Tight
Positioned
You
Tall
Prideful
Stately

A
Bronze
Statue
Silent
No expression
In your own
World
Alone
Center
Stage

You
Not
Speaking
All
The
While
We
Sit
Wait
Together
For
Our
Next
Flight

Attention All Passengers:

Official Flight Announcement:

"We have one seat available for the
earlier flight to Albuquerque."

"Right here"... she said, "I'll take that seat !"

Separate flight
Stage
Left.

Residual Sentiments

My soul to you
I shall bear no more
Although warm hugs
Felt sweet as before
Funny how one
Thinks and feels
Reflection takes its time
Then reveals
Sentiments of soul
May still reside
When fictitious though
Will subside

Not Speaking

Then what if one of us dies
And we wish we had paid more attention
Tried harder to be kind to each other
Even with both of our weird personalities
Stayed in touch
Enjoyed a friendship
No longer lovers
But good friends to each other
Heaven knows we spent many hours
Getting to know each other
Let it go to waste
Makes no sense
How many times do we individually
Think about our history together
Granted ups and downs
But real happenings
Those realities never cease
As many hours as we spent
Planning...

Now do we wonder why

I know why
It was real
We had an
Attraction
To each other
The night we met

So now
We forget?
Purposely forget?
How?
It goes like this
We get close again
You disappear
I feel hurt and get all huffy
In spite of all this
Do you think we could be friends

MAGICIAN

He can destroy you
Not purposefully
But in reality
It's a futile
Journey

You will
Sooner not
Later witness
In-person reality
Staring at you up close

As the hopefulness wanes
Your up-close discovery
Turns to a sour lime
A regret sourness
Which lives

Until you
Once again
Hear his plea
Of reconsideration
And the magic goes on

This game that is not intentional
His game of cat, mice, trap
His modus operandi
He simply has the
Skill of reality

Tricking him
To take the ride
At first pleasurable
Then setting the trap
As his deceptive feelings vanish

Pouf!

SECTION EIGHT

MEANING OF 9/11

I know a little girl
who was born on 911
her mother happy
at her birth
but why 911

Her birth was a wonderful occasion
joyous in its presence
but why then
why then
why 911

Before 911 became memorialized
it was simply a September day
and now – still - for the mother
and her precious little girl
the exact date of celebration and play

ILIANA

The poem sets the scene...
A four year old child, Iliana, was shot
and killed during a road rage incident.
The poem honors this little girl, recognizing
the heartfelt response of a loving community.

Each patron
Shakes with sadness
Tears speak
Cry out
From the depth
Within them

Grief churns
High into the rafters
It is hard to breath
Tears
Flood the surface
Beneath their feet

It suffocates you
This grief
You feel rocks
In your stomach
Ask yourself
How can this be
Days earlier
A child is laughing

Is playful
Her eyes smile
Her presence
Creates love

Now
Tears
Sorrow
Replace
The joy
In the sounds

A six year-old slides
On the pew closer to his mom
Looks up at her face
Tries to read her tears
Of heartfelt meaning
Not seen before

The unresolved
Energy of sorrow
Meets with the
Child's unsatisfied
Curious
Glance
All reach
For understanding
To make sense
Of the untimely event
As they sit
Drown in place

This small child
A lively little girl
Full of happy
Four year old energy
Full of love
Full of smiles

Lies still now
In front of them
Not in the doll house
She may have wished for
But in solemn
Ceremonious decorum

A place
A child
Should
Never
Be

Roosevelt Park

This day as I drove by Roosevelt Park
It's green green-grass so beautifully lush
With the prideful up and down hilly surface it owns
Exceeded all the theatrical beauty it could possibly summon

From my viewing
At this time on this morning
Something rare was happening
Many gigantic sprinklers were showering
All of - the entire - Roosevelt Park
Like colossal yet delicate ballet dancers
Everywhere the beautiful showering of trees
Themselves a delight in creating the giant arcs

Although no rainbow present on this day
One could imagine the intrusion of a rainbow
A rainbow the height of the trees, width of the park
The sun as it peeks through this most often shady scene

BETTY

You are everyone's Valentine
You are everyone's Christmas
You are everyone's Easter Basket
And Mother's Day
First day of Spring
A fire cracker on the 4th of July

You are Gershwin melodies
Sentimental love songs
With a side of Rock-n-Roll
The stars at their brightest
And if one star is falling
You are there to catch it

Hot Flash Look Out

Here they come
One hot flash after another
Ohhh no warning of course
Unannounced
You must simply start to de-clothe
As quickly as possible
Normally you might be cold-natured
But ohhh no
Not when the hot flashes arrive
HELP!! Get these clothes off NOW!

So take the advice
From the experienced
When you get dressed
In the morning
Especially in winter
When your choice is to be
Nice and cozy warm
WAIT a minute!
HOT FLASH Alarm!!!!!
Get peeled quick!

Got to think ahead
Plan under these
Circumstances
Else you will burn up
In no time at all
Be prepared

Learn by practice
Try a few dry runs
Afore you find yourself
Ill equipped

Make it easy to de-clothe
Which under these
Certain circumstances
Or opportunities
Could come in
Handy

Silently

May I look
Into
Your eyes
As we sit
Across
From each other
Look into
Each other's eyes
For a while

What would
Happen

Would we see
Anything more
Than we
Already know
Would our eyes
Reveal
Something
We cannot
Express

SILLY QUESTION

She watches him dance for awhile
Then could not resist
The music begins
He stands there alone
Do I dare ask you to dance
She says
Of course
We can dance
He replies

He takes her hand with style, strength
Lavish confidence and rhythm
They walk to the dance floor
The music starts to play
He asks her politely would you like
A country two step
Or a country swing?
Big smile as she says
Either would be great

First he leads a pleasing two step
Then a smooth rhythmic country swing
Adds another two-step style
"Ooh! You CAN dance".
Two BIG smiles

Thursday Night Senior Dance

I felt excitement
when I saw you
for the first time.
When we danced
during the Paul Jones Circle Dance
where it is customary
to change partners at the whistle
the whistle blew and you said
"Let's continue".

It was fun.

I began to learn
how to follow your lead.
When the band played
a very fast waltz
ending with our
sighs of relief,
we laughed
and it marked
our compatibility.

In the sweetness
of the evening
I heard you
quietly hum
with the rhythm
of the music.

Dancing 'til the band played
the last song
we wondered
could we have danced all night?

Your Dance

The gentleness
the creativity
you bring to a dance
no matter what the music
sweetness and flow
to a Night Club rhythm
style to a West Coast
a hint of the unexpected
to a country Two Step
all move toward the fun
the keeping time
the discovery
and the love
of the dance.

You've got it!

From My 8th Floor North Window

This morning
All the mountain tops
I can see clearly are
Covered with snow

Not so unusual
Except for the fact
That tomorrow
Is the first day of May

The Jemez Mountains
Win the prize
As if the whole thing
Is a competition

From my window
The Sandia Mountains
Remain dusted like a
Powdered Donut

Ready to be devoured
No doubt all the sugar
Will have disappeared
Be outshined by sunset

But the Jemez Mountain
Tops with their northern
Bent thickness of a white
Sugar cake icing thrive

SEEMING

I am happy with the times we have together
My feelings are deep with satisfaction
Being in the now seems right with only slight puzzlement
In our time together I am amazed at how comfortable we feel
Seeming obviously, the time to be quite pleasurable

How else could we possibly sit together, read, converse
Say our goodbyes and hellos for hours at a time
Time we've spent together reading our memoirs
Our hearts and minds around the individuals we are
Comes with a certain ease, empathic acceptance
A seeming understanding of each other

It doesn't seem I am only imagining this
It seems real and is often in my thoughts
If or when I learn to know your thinking
I believe I am capable of defining
My thoughts and feelings in harmony

Why

The word was unwritten
the word was being avoided
it had been heard before
the meaning experienced before
it was there staring her in the face
to no avail
not wanting to hear it again
she dismissed it at every turn
began to explore ideas
only to exclude them
in her next thoughts

she then asked herself
is it beyond my capabilities
to survive this uneasiness
this turbulence and go forward
why take this stance
is it shame
is it to save face
if so to whom
my home town
my small mid-western town
peaceful straight-laced

face my parents
my family
my friends
while carrying this burden

yet she pondered
should her own
personal growth
well-being
shame
embarrassment
be put aside

for her sons
she had to
make a livable
workable decision

what would Father Jim
advise
she sees him
every Sunday morning
she in her choir robe
he in his priesthood
she in her desperation
he in his wisdom

will she have
the courage
to meet with him
one day

yes
the talk will be
productive

she asks him
"I'd like to schedule
a visit with you
concerning
a personal matter."

they met in his study at
All Saints Episcopal Church
where they talked

Father Jim asked
a pointed question
"Don't you think
you can raise
these two boys
by yourself?"
she answered
"I hadn't thought of it
in that way".

"Of course I can
I had been only thinking
of the shame attached to it
my own shame
a second divorce."
she went forward

the divorce finalized
Greg, age 10 asked,
"Mom, is it over?"

"Is it really final now?"

"Yes Greg" she said, "It is."

"Mom, why did you take so long?"

Do You See

O say can you
If it was built
By President Obama
There is a wrecking ball
Ready to destroy it

If it has the name
Obama attached to it
Whether in deed or spoken
The edict is there
It shall be destroyed

An extinguishing of the
Obama shining lights
Affordable health care
Immigration Fairness
Shall not be seen, not heard

That history will not -
Know it, hear it, speak it
Rise only in darkness but
A black light not extinguished
Burns in honor forever and ever

It shall not be known
The accomplishments
Or shown to future generations
The applause shall not be heard
For this first young black president

Try as you may, Mr. successor
The voice, the honor, the President
The President Obama in his glory
History will show, will outshine
Outperform, outscore, out do you

The message is, Mr. current president,
In history your predecessor
Barrack Hussein Obama
Did you hear those words?
Barrack Hussein Obama
Will by far out rank you.

ADDICTS

All
Over age 65
Senior Citizens
Probably 50 of us
Can't wait
To get there
Can't wait to get to
The place on Thursday nights
That's when our drug of choice kicks in
Like clock-work
The drug takes over
Knowing these folks over time
Lends an easy guess
It is an addiction
Probably 99% of them
Bow to the need knowing the challenges
They are non-smokers
95% of them are not overweight
Yet cannot seem to override the weakness
Of this addiction called
Dancing

How I See You

You are
Kind
Thoughtful
Creative
Have a good sense of humor

You are
Intellectual
Sincere
Others-oriented
Have inner strength

You are
Clever
Patient
Playful
Have varied interests

You are
In the NOW
In the Know

With Community in mind

Quiet Curiosity

The joy in your glance
The sound of your voice
The words in what you say
The sprinkle of your thinking
The suggestions in your mannerisms
The mystery, wonderment, of your intent
The veneer, a veil, the enshrouding of emotions
How to respond or reply to the imaginary questions
How to extinguish, dismantle, these uncertainties
How to discard, invalidate, the ever present
What purpose the occasional interlude
The silent yearning for disclosure
A shy yet affectionate smile

About the Author

Carol Shelton March fell in love with New Mexico over 40 years ago. Her brother, Jerry Shelton, convinced her. She never looked back from Albuquerque. Carol came here as a single mother with two sons, Greg, age 12 and George age 6 years. Once both her sons had finished college, she attended University of New Mexico for undergraduate work before attending New Mexico Highlands University for her degree, Master of Social Work, Social Gerontology.

www.ingramcontent.com/pod-product-compliance
Lightning Source LLC
Chambersburg PA
CBHW031132090426
42738CB00008B/1064